20th Century
PERSPECTIVES

The Great Depression

David Downing

Heinemann Library
Chicago, Illinois

Designed by AMR
Illustrated by Art Construction
Originated by Dot Gradations
Printed by Wing King Tong in Hong Kong.

05 04 03 02
10 9 8 7 6 5 4 3 2

Library of Congress Cataloging-in-Publication Data
Downing, David.
    The Great Depression / David Downing.
        p. cm. -- (20th century perspectives)
    Includes bibliographical references and index.
    ISBN 1-57572-435-9 (lib. bdg.)   ISBN 1-58810-374-9 (pbk. bdg.)
        1. Depressions--1929--Juvenile literature. 2. United States--Economic
conditions--1918-1945--Juvenile literature. 3. Economic history--1918-1945--Juvenile
literature. 4. World politics--1933-1945--Juvenile literature. [1. Depressions--1929. 2.
United States--Economic conditions--1918-1945. 3. World politics--1933-1945.] I.
Title. II. Series.

E806 .D67 2001
909.82'2--dc21

                                                    00-063457

Acknowledgments
The publishers would like to thank the following for permission to reproduce photographs:
Archive Photos/Frank Driggs, p.11; Corbis, pp.15, 16, 22, 27, 32, 37; Corbis-Bettmann, p.25;
Corbis/UPI, p.14; David King, p.39; Hulton Getty, pp. 5, 4, 7, 8, 9, 10, 13, 17, 18,19, 20, 21, 23,
24, 26, 28, 29, 30, 31, 32, 33, 34, 36, 38, 40, 41, 42, 43; Imperial War Museum, p.6; The Library of
Congress, pp.12, 35.

Cover photograph reproduced with permission of Corbis.

Every effort has been made to contact copyright holders of any material reproduced in this book.
Any omissions will be rectified in subsequent printings if notice is given to the publishers.

Some words are shown in bold, **like this.** You can find out what
they mean by looking in the glossary.

Contents

An Economic Catastrophe

In early September 1929, the prices of **shares** on the **New York Stock Exchange** on **Wall Street,** which had been rising steadily for seven long years, began to slip backward. Not a lot, but enough to make some people nervous. Then prices began to inch back upward, which reassured everyone. It was just a hiccup, the buyers told each other. Soon prices would resume their relentless, and wonderfully profitable, rise.

A crowd in New York's Wall Street at the time of the Great Crash on October 29, 1929.

The Wall Street Crash

However, in late October the slip turned into a slide. A sudden wave of selling on Saturday, October 19 carried over into the following week, driving prices down and eventually causing panic selling on "Black Thursday," October 24. Nearly thirteen million shares changed hands on that day, most of them at prices far below the sellers' worst nightmares. The buyers, who thought they were scooping up bargains, would find themselves in the same dreadful situation only days later.

Over the weekend, several of the largest banks tried to halt the slide by buying shares, but by now confidence in the market had all but evaporated. Rumors of catastrophe were everywhere. The rush to sell was on, and nothing could stop it. Monday was bad, but "Black Tuesday," October 29, was the worst day of the "Great Crash." The U.S. economist J. K. Galbraith called it "the most devastating day in the history of markets." More than sixteen million shares were sold, many for practically nothing. Thousands of individual investors, and hundreds of companies that had been set up to **invest** for others, were ruined.

NEW YORK STOCK EXCHANGE

THIS WAS THE PLACE WHERE **STOCKS** AND SHARES IN U.S. BUSINESSES WERE BOUGHT AND SOLD. SHARES WERE CERTIFICATES REPRESENTING PIECES OF THE BUSINESS, WHICH ENTITLED THE HOLDER TO A SHARE OF ANY PROFITS. COMPANIES SOLD SHARES IN THEMSELVES TO FINANCE THEIR OPERATIONS. THE VALUE OF SHARES FELL DRAMATICALLY IN 1929, AS THESE FIGURES SHOW:

	MAR 28	SEP 29	NOV 29
GENERAL ELECTRIC	$129	$396	$168
GENERAL MOTORS	$140	$182	$36
WOOLWORTH	$181	$251	$52

Men who had been driven in expensive limousines and dined in New York's fanciest restaurants became beggars overnight, and there was a wave of suicides in New York's financial district. It is said that the clerks of one hotel even started asking new guests whether they needed a room for sleeping or jumping.

It soon became clear that investors were not going to be the only people to lose their livelihoods and savings as a result of the Great Crash. The tentacles of collapse spread outward from Wall Street, across the United States, across the oceans, until there was hardly a family on Earth that was left unaffected.

The effects of the Great Crash were felt globally. This march of the unemployed took place in Germany.

The Great Depression

Banks and companies failed, dragging others down with them, both in the United States and abroad. The world economy shrank in on itself. Companies all over the world went **bankrupt** or desperately cut back their costs to save themselves from bankruptcy. Wave after wave of jobs disappeared, until it seemed as if jobs were being sucked by the millions into an economic black hole of terrifying dimensions.

That black hole came to be known as the Great Depression. It lasted longer in some countries than in others, but for several years in all of them. It dominated the period between the two world wars, blighting millions of lives with poverty and hopelessness. It was at least partly responsible for the rise of **Nazism** in Germany, and for World War II (1939–1945). It would color the way most people thought about the relationship between economics and politics for the rest of the twentieth century, and still haunts us today.

It was heartbreaking

*I must have gotten calls from a dozen and a half friends who were desperate. In each case, there was no sense in loaning them the money that they would give the **broker**. Tomorrow they'd be worse off than yesterday. Suicides, left and right, made a terrific impression on me, of course. People I knew. It was heartbreaking … On Wall Street, the people walked around like zombies. It was very dark. You saw people who yesterday rode around in Cadillacs lucky now to have car fare.*

A Wall Street financier in October 1929

Consequences of World War I

World War I ended in November 1918, but its impact on the world economy would be felt for many years. The death of so many millions, the destruction of large areas of Europe, the triumph of **communism** in Russia—each would have economic consequences. So, too, would the less obvious changes, like the distortion of normal trade patterns and the changing balance of economic power between the richer nations.

The distance of the United States and Japan from the war in Europe had given their economies a chance to grow. Other countries, like Britain and France, had gone deep into debt to pay for the war, and the German economy had been weakened by the strain of continuing the struggle. One important economy, the Russian economy, had been virtually removed from the world economy by revolution and civil war. All across the world, some industries had been artificially encouraged by the needs of the war, while others, less necessary to the war effort, had struggled to survive.

If the post-war world economy was to prosper and grow, it needed time to adapt to all these changes. The first requirement was a fair and lasting peace.

Stability proves hard to achieve

There were several reasons why this proved impossible to achieve. The victorious nations were less interested in fairness than in grasping the spoils of victory. They wanted to see their victory reflected in new borders. Over the next few years many changes were made, often with little regard for the wishes of the people who actually lived in the regions concerned. This short-sighted policy encouraged many minor disputes in the 1920s, and in later years would provide the German leader Adolf Hitler with the excuses he needed to set out on a policy of conquest. The new **League of Nations**, which U.S. President Woodrow Wilson hoped would help to settle such disputes, was fatally weakened when his own country refused to join.

There were many casualties in World War I. These soldiers are learning to walk using artificial legs in 1919, one year after the end of the war.

The victorious nations also decided to demand financial compensation from the losers. These **reparations** would mostly have to be paid by an already weakened Germany. In the **Treaty of Versailles**, signed in 1919, a "war guilt clause" stated that Germany had been completely responsible for starting the war. Eventually, a huge figure, more than $32 billion, was set. The economist John Maynard Keynes, who attended the Versailles Conference as a member of the British delegation, resigned in disgust over this issue. Germany could not pay such an amount, he wrote, and making it do so would create an economic disaster. The world economy would be unbalanced still further.

This political and economic instability was made worse by the lack of economic leadership. The United States had replaced Great Britain as the most powerful player in the world economy, but U.S. political and economic leaders did not want to take on any global responsibilities. They did not think it necessary. After all, most economists at this time thought that economies did best when the politicians left them alone. These leaders thought that the world economy in 1918–1920 was like a broken bone: it simply needed time to repair itself. Few realized that the "bone" had been pushed so far out of shape by the war that surgery was needed if it was ever to heal properly.

Not the only guilty party

We are required to admit that we alone are war guilty. Such an admission on my lips would be a lie.

Senior German delegate at Versailles

At the Versailles Peace Conference of 1919, David Lloyd George, Georges Clemenceau, and Woodrow Wilson were among those present.

Ten-pin bowls

The world's economies were now so interconnected that trouble in one meant trouble in others. The Americans might wish to keep out of European quarrels, and the British and the French might be happy to see Germany in ruins, but when it came to economic matters, they were all more dependent on each other and the rest of the world than ever before. National economies were like bowling pins. A direct hit on one was likely to bring down others. A direct hit on the front pin, the United States, could bring them all down.

Europe in the 1920s

The most powerful European nations had suffered greatly from the war, but each also had its own particular problems. In Britain, a short post-war **boom** ended abruptly in the winter of 1920–1921. Higher taxes and a cutback in government spending left less money in people's pockets, and businesses found it harder to find buyers for their goods and services. Economic growth slowed dramatically, and unemployment doubled in the four months before March 1921. Wages fell and industrial disputes became more frequent. This was not the "country fit for heroes," promised by wartime **propaganda,** although **unemployment insurance** was extended to cover most of the working population.

French troops occupied Germany's Ruhr valley in January, 1923.

France had suffered more in the war. More men had been killed and injured, and large areas of the north had been destroyed by the fighting. As in Britain, French governments tried to promote stability by **balancing their budgets.** It was hard to raise taxes in France. The upper and middle classes blocked the raising of **direct taxes,** which would hit them hardest, and the working classes blocked the raising of **indirect taxes,** which would have cost them more. French governments were left to rely on the expected German **reparations** to make up the shortfall.

Crisis in Germany

Germany, virtually brought to its knees by the strain of the war, was forced to agree to the huge reparations demand from the victorious allies. The first installment of $5 billion was paid in gold, iron, coal, and timber shipments, but when the second one was due there were not enough goods left to meet it. The French refused to accept that the Germans could not pay, and in 1923 their troops occupied Germany's richest area, the industrial Ruhr valley, intending to simply take what was owed. The Germans responded by refusing to work or cooperate with the "invaders."

This enraged the French, but also created the conditions for a complete collapse in Germany. The Ruhr was now producing nothing, and many

Germany's great inflation

In 1923 I was advertising chief of a rubber factory. That was during the inflation. I had a monthly salary of 200 billion marks. We were paid twice a day, and then everybody had a half-hour's leave so that he could rush to the stores and buy something before the next quotation on the dollar came out, at which time the money would lose half its value.

A character in the 1938 novel *Three Friends*, by German author Erich Maria Remarque

Children in Germany play with worthless money during the Great Inflation of 1923.

more workers were looking to the government for support. The politicians tried to make up the difference by printing money, and **inflation** spiralled out of control. A loaf of bread that cost two-thirds of a mark, the German currency, in 1918, and 250 marks in January 1923, cost 201 billion marks by November of that year. German money had become virtually worthless.

Such a situation was clearly not in anyone's interests. If the Germans could not pay reparations to the British and French, they in turn would not be able to pay off their war debts to the United States. So over the next year a financial deal, the Dawes Plan, was worked out. The United States would loan Germany enough money to rebuild its economy and pay reparations to France and Britain. These countries would then be able to pay their debts.

A hopeful period

At first, this arrangement proved very successful. In Europe, the years between 1925 and 1929 were marked by growing prosperity and increasing political stability. In many countries, unemployment remained high, and the threat of inflation still persisted, but the overall economic picture seemed to be brightening at last. Only a few people knew how dependent the whole European economy was on the health of the U.S. economy. Stresemann, the German Foreign Minister, was one of them. "Germany is in fact dancing on the edge of a volcano," he said in 1929. If the Americans demanded the repayment of their loans, he added, then a large section of the German economy would collapse.

The United States in the 1920s

During World War I, the U.S. economy had expanded to fill the gap left by lower production of many goods in Europe. Once the war was over, this **demand** dropped, and for a brief period the economy went into **recession.** These difficulties were one cause of the social unrest that followed the war. In 1919–1920, there were race riots and disputes among workers in the police, coal, and steel industries. A great fear of **communist** influence in the United States created a "Red Scare." Thousands of people were arrested, mostly for short periods.

Workers assemble cars on the Ford assembly line in Dearborn, Michigan, March 1928.

A booming economy

Warren Harding became president in 1921, the first of three successive **Republican** presidents. Over the next eight years, he and his successors—Calvin Coolidge (1923–1929) and Herbert Hoover (1929–1933)—followed policies that favored business. Income tax and taxes on business were reduced, while **indirect taxes** were raised. It became easier to borrow money. **Tariffs** on industrial **imports** were also raised, protecting U.S. industries from outside competition.

These policies created an industrial **boom,** which was reinforced by the growth of new industries based on new technologies. The automobile industry was the most important. Its expansion helped fuel the growth of other industries, like steel, rubber, and glass, whose products were used in the construction of cars. There was also great growth in the household appliance industry, as families rushed to buy new refrigerators, radios, and vacuum cleaners. For many Americans, this was a time of steadily increasing prosperity. Workers' pay doubled during the decade.

Of course, not everyone shared in this prosperity. Farmers, helped by new agricultural technology, were producing too much, and prices for their crops remained low. The Republicans' pro-business policies, though good at encouraging growth, were also widening the gap between rich and poor, and the poorest Americans, many of whom belonged to ethnic minorities, were having a difficult time.

African Americans set up groups to campaign for reform. They asked the government for help in improving their general situation. They also asked for laws against **lynching** and new voting rights. The requests were ignored.

A dangerous optimism

For the majority of Americans, the 1920s were a time of great optimism. The decade became known as the "roaring 20s," the "age of excess," and the "jazz age." There were new inventions, the first flights across oceans, movies with sound, new music. The world was changing so fast, and all for the better. There seemed no reason why prosperity should ever end with no limits to what Americans could achieve or own or do.

As the decade went by, this sense of optimism encouraged two dangerous states of mind. One was the feeling that nothing could go wrong, and that therefore nothing had to be done to guard against disaster. President Coolidge's 1928 State of the Union address was a good example of this. The second state of mind was a sort of wild blindness, a willingness to take what, in any other time, would have been considered foolish chances. The best example of this was the mad rush to make money on the stock market.

Louis Armstrong, called "The man who put the 'jazz' into 'jazz age,'" is shown with his band, "Hot Five," in 1925.

Official optimism

No Congress of the United States ever assembled, on surveying the state of the Union, has met with a more pleasing prospect than that which appears at the present time. The great wealth created by our enterprise and industry, and saved by our economy, has had the widest distribution among our own people, and has gone out in a steady stream to serve the charity and business of the world. The requirements of existence have passed beyond the standard of necessity into the region of luxury. The country can regard the present with satisfaction and anticipate the future with optimism.

From President Coolidge's State of the Union address, 1928

The Great Crash

The Florida land boom

The widespread belief that every American could now get rich received its first setback in the Florida land **boom** of 1924–1926. Land in Florida was very cheap at the beginning of the decade, but as the state grew more popular for vacations and retirement homes, prices began to rise. Land buyers in Florida only had to come up with ten percent of the price for a "binder," which was a piece of paper giving them the exclusive right to buy that piece of land. When the value of the land went up they could sell this "binder" and make a big profit, without ever needing to pay the other 90 percent.

This system worked well, and everyone made a profit, as long as the price of Florida land kept rising. However, by 1926, most of the good land had been sold, a hurricane had done great damage to the state, and prices had begun to fall. Those at the end of the chain, who had paid over-high prices for binders, found that they owed ten percent of the price on land that was now worth much less than the ten percent they had already paid out.

Up, up, and away

Another version of the same sad story would be repeated a few years later on **Wall Street.** The price of a **share** was supposed to reflect the well-being of a company. If it was a big company, with high expected profits, then generally the price of the shares would be high. But such exact calculations were often hard to determine, and other factors, from rumors to the health of the economy as a whole, could influence share prices.

If it was expected that prices would keep on rising, then some people would buy shares just to sell them again a little later and pocket the profit. These people, who were not interested in the long-term health of the companies whose shares they bought, were more like **speculators** than investors. In the United States in the late 1920s, confidence was so high, and the chances of growing rich by gambling on the stock exchange so good, that a fever of speculation took hold.

Things were made easy for the speculators. As with land in Florida, people were allowed to buy with a ten percent deposit. In the stock market, it was called "buying on the margin." In addition, investment **trusts** were formed that sold shares in themselves and used the money they received to buy other shares, often in other investment trusts. There were 300 of these trusts in 1927, and 750 only two years later. The price of shares kept going up, but each day the price bore less and less relation to anything in the real world of work and production.

The bubble bursts

In that world, there were signs as early as 1928 that the boom was coming to an end. The farmers were still in trouble, and the widening gap between rich and poor was now affecting industrial production. By this time, the rich had bought all the new appliances they needed, and there were too many poor people who could not afford to buy any. Since countries around the world had responded to U.S. **tariffs** with tariffs of their own, the surplus U.S. goods could not be sold overseas.

It was only a matter of time before this economic downturn began to raise doubts about the price of shares. The first doubters sold their shares.

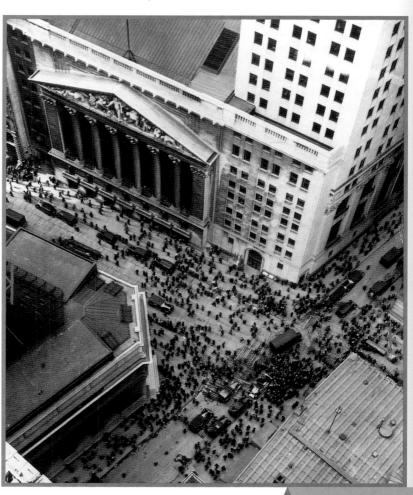

Panic in Wall Street followed news of the Crash on October 29, 1929.

Slowly at first, but soon with dizzying speed, the fever of buying turned into a fever of selling. In a few days in October 1929, the stock market on Wall Street came crashing down. By mid-November it had lost 40 percent of its value, and many thousands of investors had lost everything.

They were the first victims of this man-made disaster, but far from the last. Over the next few years, there would be millions more, and they would be found in almost every country on the planet.

13

From Crash to Depression

Historians and economists have argued about the relationship between the Great Crash and the Great Depression. All agree that it was not a simple matter of one causing the other. The existing depression was partly to blame for the **stock market** crash, but the crash was then responsible for the depression turning out much deeper and longer than it would otherwise have been.

It may seem strange that a collapse of prices on the stock market could have had such a huge impact on the rest of the economy. After all, only about 4 million people out of a U.S. population of more than 100 million owned **shares,** and fewer than half that number were serious players on the stock exchange. But the rippling effects of the Crash were soon spreading across the United States, bringing disaster in their wake. Weaker businesses were swept away and even some of the strongest had trouble surviving.

The collapse of confidence

The first thing the Great Crash destroyed was confidence. No one wanted to risk **investing** in an economy that was on the slide. On the contrary, most people were desperate to get back any money they had already invested while that was still possible. The same was true of simple bank deposits. Many banks had lost heavily in the stock market crash, and the customers of all banks were now eager to take out their money at the first hint of trouble. It only needed one person to start a "run" on any particular bank, and by nightfall the vaults would be empty and the bank out of business. There were more than 11,000 such failures in the United States in the period 1929–1933.

The people standing in line outside this bank in New York wanted to withdraw their money. The bank was in the hands of the State Examiner and was closed for 24 hours.

In addition, the banks demanded repayment of loans. People who had borrowed money to buy their homes, and businessmen who had borrowed money to start up a new business or expand an existing one, suddenly found their homes repossessed or their businesses **bankrupt.**

Chain reaction

All this was happening to an economy that had been slowing down even before the stock market crashed. In many industries and in farming, there had already been too much production, and now the gap between what people could buy and what was being made widened at breakneck speed. Businesses in difficulty laid off workers, swelling the growing army of the unemployed. With fewer wages coming in, people spent less on goods, which put more businesses in trouble and created even more unemployment. People who still had jobs were often forced to accept lower wages, which meant they could not buy as much as before.

Borrowed time

After two years the jazz age seems as far away as the days before the War. It was borrowed time anyhow – the whole upper tenth of a nation living with the insouciance [lack of concern] of grand dukes and the casualness of chorus girls.

Author F. Scott Fitzgerald, 1931

The U.S. economy seemed caught in a downward spiral. Between 1929 and the end of 1932, investment fell by half, industrial production fell by 43 percent, and the total value of stocks by around 80 percent. Unemployment rose to 25 percent: At its peak in 1933, one out of every four people was out of work. At one point in 1932, the jobless total was going up by 12,000 people each day. That year there were 23,000 suicides, the worst such year in U.S. history.

President Hoover, shown here at his desk in the White House, believed the economy would sort itself out.

The failure of government

Government and business leaders did little to put things right. President Hoover thought the economy would sort itself out, and that intervention would do more harm than good. Business leaders promised to keep up wages, prices, investments, and employment levels, and so halt the slide, but they failed to do this. Each company acted in its own interests. With the government unwilling to intervene, there was no one to enforce the interests of the whole country.

When persuasion failed, the government did nothing. It would neither act to right the situation nor help those suffering the consequences. Hoover refused to consider relief payments to either farmers or the millions of unemployed. He preferred clinging to the belief that a new period of prosperity was just around the corner.

From the U.S. to the Rest of the World

Not all the losses on **Wall Street** had been American. As **share** prices had risen, many European financial institutions, such as banks, had been unable to resist such sensational profits, and they too suffered badly in the Great Crash. This would have been serious in itself for Europe and the rest of the world. The fact that the world economy had been set up like a row of dominoes by the post-war economic arrangements made things even worse.

Free food was distributed to the poor in Austria.

Europe . . .

Germany was the first domino to fall. It had borrowed huge sums of money from the United States to finance its own economic recovery and the payment of war **reparations** to Britain and France. More than half of these were short-term loans, which had to be renewed every few months. After the Great Crash, U.S. banks, desperate to survive, simply demanded their money back. All over Germany, companies either cut back or went **bankrupt,** and unemployment began rising, from just over 1 million in September 1929 to more than 6 million in January 1933.

This was bad news for Britain and France in many ways. The crisis in Germany meant popular support increased for the **communists** and Adolf Hitler's **Nazi** Party. Germany ended its reparations payments. President Hoover rubbed salt in this wound by refusing to cancel the British and French war debts to the United States.

Like business leaders in the United States, the world's most powerful governments seemed incapable of seeing beyond their own short-term interests, when their long-term interests would have been much better served by working together. For example, as the months went by, they all started raising existing **tariffs** to protect their own industries. This soon led to a reduction in world trade, making matters worse for everybody.

The number of unemployed in Britain, which had been above one million since the war, rose considerably. France, which had a more rural economy, was less affected at first, but here too the jobless total moved upwards. It was the same story all over Europe. As **credit** became harder and harder to get, and as the world economy weakened and businesses failed, the streets were filled with people made idle through no fault of their own.

. . . and beyond

In the rest of the world, it was the falling price of **primary products** that did most of the damage. Many of these prices were already falling

before the Great Crash due to worldwide over-production, but the weakening of the world economy sent them plummeting. Every nation that relied on selling such goods suffered.

In Australia, the price of wheat and wool fell by around 55 percent between 1928 and 1931, and a severe drought in 1929 made matters worse. The total value of Australia's exports was almost halved during these few years. The collapse in 1930 of the U.S. demand for Japanese silk caused great hardship in the Japanese countryside, and countries like Brazil, Ceylon, and Cuba were hit by falling world prices for coffee, tea, and sugar.

Almost half of Japan's farmers relied on silk production to supplement their low income from other crops.

As these industries suffered, so the ripple effect was felt throughout the economy. A small farmer in a far corner of India, pleading with his village moneylender for more time to pay his debts, probably had no idea that a world credit shortage was responsible for his moneylender's unusual refusal to take payment in crops. He would doubtless have had a hard time believing that his own struggle to make ends meet had suddenly grown more difficult because a few people had been overcome with gambling fever in lands beyond his horizon.

In the Cities

For most people, the central reality of the Great Depression was unemployment. Millions were unemployed or dependent on those who were, millions more were afraid of being so. In 1930, few countries paid any **benefits** to the unemployed, and those that were paid were often inadequate. Millions of people had to rely on charity, either in the form of relief payouts from governments that often had humiliating conditions attached to them, or in the form of food and other necessary items distributed by the charity organizations.

Even in Washington, D.C., there were "Hoovervilles" in the 1930s.

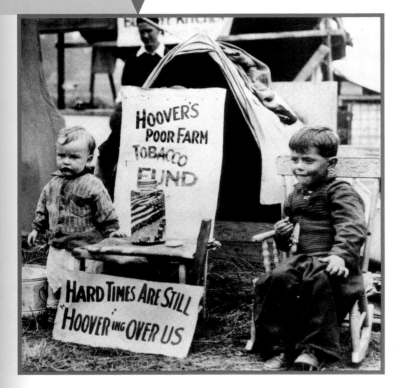

Homeless

Without wages, many people found it impossible to afford rent or **mortgage** payments, and were thrown out of their homes. All over the world, **shanty towns** sprang up on empty sites, full of makeshift homes made from whatever materials the homeless could find. Others had no roof at all. In the summer of 1931, several hundred women slept each night in Chicago's parks. Fifty-four men, arrested for sleeping in a New York subway, were overjoyed to find that the police were too busy to process them. In jail, they would receive several good meals and a warm bed for the night.

Many of the homeless abandoned their hometowns and cities, taking to the road in the hope of finding a job elsewhere.

One young couple

*Attracted by smoke from the chimney of a supposedly empty summer cottage near Awana Lake, Constable Simon Glaser found a young couple starving. After three days without food, the wife, who is twenty-three years old, was hardly able to walk. The couple had been unemployed since their formerly wealthy employer lost his money, and several days ago they **invested** all they had, except 25 cents for food, in bus fare to this region in search of work. Finding none, they went to the cottage, preferring to starve rather than beg. They said they had resigned themselves to dying together.*

Report in the *New York Times*, Christmas Day 1931

In 1932, there were more than 25,000 U.S. families and about 200,000 young men wandering around the country in this way, spending their nights in railroad cars, campsites, and city shelters. In Australia, such transients were called "soldiers of despair."

Hungry

Many people spent much of their time hungry. In New York City, which had better relief services than most, one in five children was suffering from **malnutrition** in 1932. Newspapers published recipes using the cheapest ingredients, but many people could not afford even those. There were long lines for the bread and soup, which were given out by charity organizations, and in the worst areas, people rummaged through gutters and garbage dumps looking for scraps of food.

Angry

In the face of such a human calamity, it was only natural that those who found themselves badly affected should feel angry. As the months went by, with no sign that matters were improving, many people expressed this anger however they could. Most blamed their governments, and these, whether democratic or republican, had a hard time holding on to power. In the United States, President Hoover became so identified with the Depression that he lost any real chance of winning the next election. The shanty towns of the unemployed became known as "Hoovervilles," and the food dished out in soup kitchens as "Hoover stew."

An appeal

I am persuaded to write to you, concerning aid to unemployment. I hope this movement will be speeded up so people in Pottstown will feel and know results before Cold weather comes upon us, the struggling starving working class undernourished Men, women and children. It really is alarming that this so-called prosperous nation that we must suffer on account of a few men seeking power and rule . . . I am one of the men out of work but the rich don't care so long as they have full and plenty.

Anonymous letter to President Hoover, October 1930

Unemployed workers eat a meal in a Chicago soup kitchen, 1930.

Protest

Fighting back

Protests often went far beyond name-calling. People all over the world were prepared to break the law if their own and their families' survival depended on it. Groups of unemployed people would often attack grocery stores, grabbing what they could from the shelves before the police turned up. Crowds would surround representatives of the authorities when they arrived at a particular home to cut off services, take back goods, or evict the occupants. Often there would be violence, but sometimes events would take a comic turn, as protesters returned through the back door those items that the representatives of the authorities had removed through the front. As time went by neighborhoods grew more organized, and "Unemployed Councils" were formed to help those in need, supplying everything from new shoes to legal advice.

There was also increasing trouble at workplaces, and on many occasions this turned to violence. In the summer of 1931, in the coalfields of Ohio, Pennsylvania, and Kentucky, the owners used private armies to set up a reign of terror against the angry workers. In Dearborn, Michigan, in March 1932, four men were shot dead during a demonstration. Business and government leaders feared that the whole industrial situation could get out of hand. Many of them would later support President Roosevelt's answer to the crisis, the New Deal, because they feared that the only alternative was a revolution.

Soldiers of the "Bonus Army" camped out in sight of the Capitol, Washington D.C., 1932.

The Bonus Army

In the United States, the most famous demonstration was that mounted by the "Bonus Army" in Washington, D.C. This "army" was composed of World War I veterans who had, after that war, been promised a financial bonus in far-off 1945. By 1932, many of them were so poor that they asked for the payment to be brought forward. More than 20,000 veterans made their way to Washington to protest on the steps of the U.S. Capitol.

In June 1932, they set up a "Hooverville," or **shanty town,** within sight of the White House, and demanded that **Congress** pay out their bonuses. When Congress refused to pay, the veterans refused to leave, and President Hoover decided to evict them.

Four troops of cavalry, four companies of infantry, a machine-gun squadron, and six tanks were assembled near the White House and then used to clear and destroy the veterans' camp. Three of the U.S. Army officers involved—Douglas MacArthur, Dwight Eisenhower, and George Patton—would later play prominent roles in World War II.

The Jarrow March

In Great Britain, the best-known demonstration of the time was a peaceful one. In the northeastern town of Jarrow, the closing of industries had left most men without work, and in the fall of 1936, several hundred of the unemployed walked 300 miles (483 km) to London to ask the government to create more jobs. The "Jarrow Marchers" received much sympathy from the general population, but little more than empty promises of help from the British government.

The Jarrow Marchers pass through a small English town.

In the United States and Britain, the **democratic** political systems, with some minor changes, survived this rising tide of protest, and the revolution feared by a few failed to materialize. In other countries, the banner of protest was carried by more extremist political groups, such as the **Nazis,** and when these came to power, the changes would be more fundamental and far more dangerous.

Jarrow

Wherever we went there were men hanging about, not scores of them but hundreds and hundreds of them. The men wore the drawn masks of prisoners of war. A stranger from a distant civilization, observing the condition of the place and its people, would have arrived at once at the conclusion that Jarrow had deeply offended some celestial Emperor of the island and was now being punished.

The English writer J. B. Priestley, after a visit to Jarrow

On the Land

A world problem

In most countries during the Great Depression, life in the countryside was as difficult as life in the cities. Times had been hard since World War I. New technologies had encouraged greater production, but since demand had not risen at the same rate, prices for most crops had started to fall. In order to maintain their incomes, farmers had produced even more, but this, of course, brought the prices down still further. It grew much harder to export the extra crops because each country raised its import taxes to protect its own farmers.

A U.S. farmer pours away milk that he cannot sell at a profit.

Many farmers were forced to borrow money, but as prices kept falling it grew harder to keep up with repayments. During the Great Depression, few banks could afford to wait for their money. As a result, one in twenty American farmers lost their farms between 1930 and 1933. In some states, like Iowa, the proportion was as high as one in eight.

Tenant farmers were even worse off. They often relied on their landlords to keep them during the winter; the following summer they would pay them back in crops. However, as the Depression took hold, and the crops came to be worth less and less, landlords became unwilling to support their tenants in this way. Many tenant farmer families took to the road, and some starved.

Different responses

In some areas, farmers tried to take matters into their own hands. In Iowa, members of the local Farmers Union blocked roads and attacked trucks carrying food to the town. They hoped that by creating shortages they would drive up prices. As in the cities, people quickly gathered to try to prevent friends from being evicted.

Some simply gave way to despair. One American sheep farmer found that it would cost him $1.10 to ship each of his 3,000 sheep to the market. He would receive only $1 per sheep in return. Rather than watch them starve to death, he cut their throats and threw them in a canyon.

The situation was similar in all the countries that had relied on exporting agricultural products. As prices fell, crops were often left to wither in the fields because it cost more to harvest and transport them than they were worth. Farmers tried to cut costs by reverting to the old ways of working. In Australia for example, horses were brought back to replace tractors, and the use of chemical fertilizers was drastically cut back.

The occupants of this Colorado dust–bowl farm had not yet joined the exodus to California.

The U.S. dust bowls

In the United States, several years of poor weather conditions on the Great Plains made the situation still worse. Pockets of drought in 1930–31 spread further in 1932 and intensified in 1933. By 1934 a huge area covering a dozen states was affected. The **topsoil,** which the long grasses had held firm for thousands of years, had been exposed in the 1920s by overcultivation and overgrazing, and now, dried out by the drought, it simply blew away, leaving "dust bowls" where farm land had been.

The dust bowls were not caused by the Great Depression, but the streams of **migrants** heading north and west to escape it have become one of the lasting images of the time. The hardships they endured, as told so movingly in John Steinbeck's novel *The Grapes of Wrath*, were certainly made much worse by the wider Depression affecting the United States as a whole.

A sin and a crime

And a homeless hungry man, driving the road with his wife beside him and his thin children in the backseat, could look at the fallow [uncultivated] fields which might produce food but not profit, and that man could know how a fallow field is a sin and the unused land a crime against thin children . . .

And in the south he saw the golden oranges hanging on the trees, the little golden oranges on the dark green trees; and guards with shotguns patrolling the lines so a man might not pick an orange for a thin child, oranges to be dumped if the price was low . . .

from *The Grapes of Wrath* by John Steinbeck

Roosevelt's New Deal

A new president

When the **Democratic Party's** Franklin Delano Roosevelt became president in March 1933, unemployment was still soaring, and a collapse of confidence in the banks had led most of them to close their doors. Roosevelt acted decisively. There was relief money for the hungry and the homeless, and help with refinancing **mortgages** for those in danger of losing their houses and farms. To ensure that there was no repeat of the Great Crash, stricter regulations were introduced for banks and the **stock market.** Some accused him of behaving like a dictator, but most people were only too happy that at long last their government was doing something about the Depression.

Getting the United States back to work

Before his election, Roosevelt had promised "a New Deal for the American people," and during the **hundred days** he introduced a series of new laws to bring this about. The agencies created to see that these laws were enacted came to be known by their initials, and were called the "Alphabet Agencies."

By the end of summer 1933, 300,000 CCC volunteers were engaged in a variety of tasks, like those here planting trees.

The Civilian Conservation Corps (CCC) paid young men $1 a day to do public work. The new **Public Works** Administration (PWA) was formed to oversee the building of new houses, dams, and hospitals, the electrification of railroads, and even the construction of a new sewage system for Chicago.

The PWA mostly employed skilled workers, but the Civil Works Administration (CWA) and the later Works Progress Administration (WPA) also took on unskilled workers. Some of the jobs they provided, like road-building and cleaning up schools, were clearly useful, while others, like sweeping up leaves and researching strange subjects for no obvious reason, seemed less so. But for most of those involved, any sort of work was better than none.

There was also help for those who still had jobs. The National Recovery Administration (NRA) tried to set up codes of conduct in industry which would, eventually, benefit everybody. In return for giving its workers fair wages and the right to join unions, companies could use the NRA's symbol—a blue eagle with the motto "we do our part"—as part of their advertising campaigns. In rural areas, the Agricultural Adjustment Act (AAA) allowed the government to pay farmers to produce less. This gave them a basic income and pushed up prices.

As part of the New Deal, the Tennessee Valley Authority generated thousands of jobs including building 21 dams.

The TVA

The most famous of the "Alphabet Agencies," which oversaw the biggest government project of the entire New Deal, was the TVA, or Tennessee Valley Authority. The large area drained by the Tennessee River, which covered several states, including Tennessee, Kentucky, Alabama, and Georgia, and several others, had already been identified by Roosevelt as "the nation's number one economic problem." The TVA, by building 21 large dams and starting a massive **reforestation** program, would prevent the annual floods, help conserve the vanishing **topsoil,** and generate enormous amounts of **hydroelectric power.**

Many of the measures introduced in 1933 had their limitations. The AAA-sponsored destruction of crops helped many farmers, but it greatly angered the hungry and did nothing for those farm workers who didn't own land. The public works programs provided some jobs, but unemployment remained high for many years. The system as a whole was not changed.

The overall effect was, however, positive. People had more money to spend, and the economy began to grow again. After four terrible years, it seemed as if the United States was finally on the mend.

A letter to Roosevelt

Dear Mr President,
This is just to tell you that everything is all right now. The man you sent found our house all right and we went down the bank with him and the mortgage can go on a while longer. You remember I wrote about losing the furniture too. Well, your man got it back for us. I never heard of a president like you, Mr Roosevelt. Mrs ... and I are old folks and don't amount to much, but we are joined with those millions of others in praying for you every night. God bless you, Mr Roosevelt.

letter to the White House, 1934

Making the New Deal Work

Though necessary, the measures President Roosevelt introduced in 1933 were a great shock to many Americans. The **federal** government had never intervened so directly in the country's economic and political life. There were those who thought Roosevelt should have gone even farther —people like the Louisiana politician Huey Long and radio broadcaster Father Charles Coughlin—but most of the opposition to his New Deal came from those who believed that he had gone too far. These opponents believed that government should do as little as possible to interfere with the way the **free market** operated.

Although Roosevelt's policies were not popular with industrialists, most people appreciated his programs.

Roosevelt v. The Supreme Court

Among Roosevelt's most prominent opponents were many industrialists who believed that too much power was being given to their employees. Men like Henry Ford refused to sign up with the NRA, and many of the bosses who did sign were inclined to pick and choose which parts of the agreement they carried out. These opponents were mostly the people who had benefited from the **Republicans'** probusiness policies in the 1920s, and they still had support in **Congress** and the Supreme Court.

When a New York company was accused by the NRA of selling diseased chickens, it took the case all the way to the Supreme Court, which ruled in its favor. The federal government, the judges said, had no right to interfere in the poultry business.

This was the beginning of a long struggle between Roosevelt and his opponents. Over the next few years, fourteen other cases were brought before the Supreme Court, and nine of them went against the president. The AAA was declared illegal on the grounds that the states, and not the federal government, should be giving help to farmers. The federal government was only supposed to be responsible for business and industries that affected all the states, the judges said. The whole New Deal seemed in danger of being undone.

A second New Deal

Roosevelt fought back by introducing a second wave of laws. These created agencies to replace those that the Supreme Court had declared illegal, and virtually amounted to a second New Deal. The Wagner Act, which succeeded the NRA, gave workers the right to join and form unions. The Soil Conservation Act, which replaced the AAA, allowed the federal government to use care of the environment as its reason for supporting farmers. The Social Security Act broke new ground, setting up national systems of pensions, help for the disabled, and **unemployment insurance.** Never again, it was hoped, would Americans be reduced to the poverty of the Great Depression's early years.

Roosevelt guessed that, left to its own devices, the Supreme Court would probably decide that this second New Deal was no more legal than the first. He countered this threat with another, promising to pack the Court with new judges if there was any attempt to block his measures. As a result, there was none.

In 1937, he decided that the worst of the Depression was over and cut federal spending. This decision, which coincided with a downturn in world trade, proved a serious mistake. Industrial production and the **stock market** fell sharply, and unemployment climbed back past the 10 million mark during 1938. People expressed their dissatisfaction by giving the Republicans a majority in Congress in that year's elections, a result that effectively closed the door on any further New Deal legislation. The Great Depression was no longer "great," but unemployment would remain high until the U.S. economy was boosted by the outbreak and spread of a new world war.

This New Deal era poster issued by the Works Progress Administration celebrates the value of work.

Roosevelt's pledge

I see millions denied education, recreation and the opportunity to better their lot and the lot of their children. I see millions lacking the means to buy the products of farm and factory and by their poverty denying work and productiveness to many other millions. I see one third of the nation ill-housed, ill-clad and ill-nourished. It is not despair that I paint you in this picture. I paint it for you in hope – because the Nation proposes to paint it out.

from Roosevelt's second Inaugural Speech January 1937

Great Britain and France

The Depression in Britain

Britain's Labor Government was just as unwilling to intervene decisively in the economy as Hoover's **Republican** administration in the United States had been. Economists like John Maynard Keynes, who pleaded for a **public works** program to stimulate the economy, were ignored. Instead, the British government persisted with traditional policies. If the nation had a **balanced budget,** its leaders claimed, the situation would right itself. If times were hard, the country needed to tighten its belt, not go on a spending spree. In July 1931, a report recommended cutting unemployment **benefits** and other government expenditure. Keynes called it "the most foolish document" he had ever read.

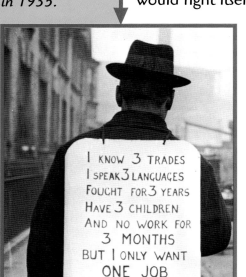

Britain's situation was worsened by the end of German **reparations** payments and the spread of **protectionism,** following the introduction of higher U.S. **tariffs** in 1930. The British government responded by ceasing payments on its war debt to the United States and introducing higher tariffs of its own for nonempire trade. An imperial conference was held in Ottawa, Canada, in 1932 to promote free trade inside the British empire, but the different countries and colonies were all too busy safeguarding their own interests to agree on very much.

In Britain, unemployment continued to rise. A new national government introduced cuts in benefits and other spending, and carried on trying to balance the budget, but with little effect. The Depression was felt everywhere, but a few regions such as Northeast England, Scotland's Clyde valley, South Wales, and Lancashire were the most badly hit. Here, there was much suffering, with whole towns like Jarrow often devastated by the closure of one large industry. But the places were a long way from London and the government. In the rest of England, stable wages and lower prices meant many people were actually better off in the 1930s.

The Depression in France

The Depression came more slowly to France. The economy was less dependent on trade than Britain's, there was less industry that could be affected, and the impact of rising unemployment could be softened for the local inhabitants by sending home the many workers who came from surrounding countries. It was not until 1932–33 that the country was seriously affected.

The lost millions

Nothing to do with time; nothing to spend; nothing to do tomorrow nor the day after; nothing to wear; can't get married. A living corpse; a unit of the spectral [ghostly] army of three million lost men.

Hands in pockets, shoulders hunched, he would slink around the by-streets to the billiard hall, glad to be somewhere out of the way of the public gaze, any place where there were no girls to see him in his threadbare jacket and patched overalls.

The unemployed hero of Walter Greenwood's 1933 novel *Love on the Dole*

When this happened, French governments tried to follow the same traditional policies as the British. Unfortunately, their political system, based on **proportional representation,** made it harder for them to take unpopular action. No party could ever gain an absolute majority in the French Parliament, and so government quickly followed government, with none able to really tackle the economic situation. The reputation of government itself was damaged, and there was growing support for extremist parties. By the end of the 1930s, France was a deeply divided nation.

The political consequences

There was no New Deal before World War II in either Britain or France. This was partly because there was less need for one due to better social benefits in these countries than in the United States, but more because of the political culture. Britain's backward-looking political parties had no sense of adventure, and the French political system made it virtually impossible for any party to push through such a daring program of change.

French workers from the north staged a hunger march in 1933.

The economies of both countries were eventually stimulated back into growth by **rearmament** programs and the general recovery of the world economy. But the absence of anything resembling a New Deal reflected a lack of confidence in the political leaderships of both countries, and this would have a disastrous effect on their dealings with a Germany that was rising up again.

The World at Large

In the 1930s, most of the world beyond Europe and North America was still ruled by several European countries. Even those countries in Africa, Asia, and Latin America not ruled, directly or indirectly, by one of these European powers had little real independence in economic matters. When it came to trade, they were **colonies** in everything but name.

These countries and colonies sold food and raw materials to Europe and North America and used the money they received to buy manufactured goods. Until the end of World War I, this seemed a reasonably fair arrangement, but in the 1920s, the price of food and raw materials fell in relation to the price of industrial goods. With the onset of the Great Depression, this gap grew even wider, pushing the interests of the trading partners farther and farther apart.

Low prices and unemployment led to this riot in Melbourne, Australia, in 1933.

Australia

Australia's situation was typical. Wool and wheat prices fell. The economy shrank. Unemployment soared. Men marched, **shanty towns** went up, violence erupted. As elsewhere, some people prospered amidst the general gloom.

Because the economy was so entangled with that of Britain, the government was forced to follow the same mistaken policies of wage reduction and spending cuts. The worst was over by 1933, and there was even compensation in the fact that new industries had sprung up to produce those goods that the country could no longer afford to import. The Great Depression made Australians eager to assert their economic independence, and more capable of being so.

On instructions from owners, property managers had been throwing bankrupt people out of their homes. People took the law into their own hands in retaliation:

It was late shopping night and at a quarter to nine there were two of us outside each of nine [real] estate agents in Richmond. One chap in each group had a watch and they were all synchronized. At a quarter to nine, "Bang!" We wrecked every estate agent's window in Richmond with lumps of bluemetal. There was hell to pay the next morning. The papers were full of it.

A member of the Unemployed Workers Movement in Richmond, Australia

India, Africa, and Latin America

India was still a British colony, and its economy was run by the colonial power. When British and Indian interests differed, there was no doubt as to whose would come first. At the Ottawa Conference, 10 Indian products were given **preferential access** to the British market, while 162 British products were given similar access to the Indian market. In India itself, the British simply tried to **balance the budget,** as they had at home. There was no help for rich farmers, landlords, and money-lenders who had been hit by the Great Depression, and from this time on, many would join the vast ranks of the poor in supporting the Indian Congress Party and its struggle for independence.

Mahatma Gandhi is shown on the left with other leaders of the Indian Congress Party leadership, 1938.

In Africa, the Depression was first felt in those sectors of the economy such as the mines, plantations, and **cash-crop** areas that were most closely linked to the colonial homelands in Europe. Banks cut back on their operations. Companies cut wages and fired workers. The prices paid to growers dropped. As the continent's people had less money to spend, so the whole economy shrank, leaving only **subsistence farmers** unaffected. European enterprises were hit by a rise in the number of strikes, and there were boycotts of foreign stores.

The same economic processes occurred in Latin America, where most nations were at least, in theory, independent. But in matters of trade, their governments were as powerless as local colonial administrations. These countries were also much more vulnerable to popular discontent. In Brazil and Argentina, governments that had been in power since World War I were toppled by Depression uneasiness.

All over the world beyond Europe and North America there was disillusion with a colonial system that had so obviously failed to protect its peoples from the impact of the Great Depression. This disillusion would provide the fuel for numerous independence movements, which sprang into existence during and after World War II.

Germany and Japan

The rise of the Nazis

In Germany throughout the period 1930–1932, a succession of governments tried to deal with the worsening economic situation in much the same way as the British and French. They cut services, **benefits,** and wages to try to **balance the budget.** When these policies failed, the German people, who had already suffered extreme hardships in the 1920s, showed that they were prepared to take desperate measures. As unemployment went up, so did the number of votes cast for Hitler's **Nazi** Party.

Hitler blamed foreigners for Germany's plight, the western powers for imposing such a harsh peace in 1918, and the Jews within Germany, who he wrongly claimed were manipulating the economy for their own selfish ends. In the July 1932 elections, the Nazis won more votes than any other party, and in January 1933, Hitler became Chancellor, the leader of the German government. By mid-1934, he had effectively turned Germany from a **democracy** into a **dictatorship.**

Hitler's economic success

Hitler opened the first stretch of the highway between Frankfurt am Maine and Darmstadt, May 19, 1935.

More by luck than judgment, the Nazis adopted economic policies that proved successful in dealing with the Depression in Germany. Since they wanted their control over the country to be complete, they were much more willing to intervene directly in the economy than the British or French. They were also determined to restore German pride and military strength, which involved spending huge amounts of public money on the construction of highways and a **rearmament** program. This high spending soon got the German economy moving again. Hitler quickly pointed out that his party had succeeded where his predecessors, and Britain and France, had failed. German pride had been restored, while the reputation of democracy was further damaged.

All that stood between Germany and a full recovery from her postwar troubles was the settlement imposed by the **Treaty of Versailles.** Hitler's economic successes won him the support he needed at home to start to undo that settlement. His massive rearmament program would eventually give him the means to break the treaty by force.

Japanese answers

The Japanese had also been hit hard by the Depression. They were especially weakened in the countryside, where the dramatic slump in the world silk and rice markets created areas of desperate poverty. Between 1929 and 1931, the Japanese government followed the British, French, and Germans in pursuing traditional policies, with much the same results. In late 1931, a new Minister of Finance, Takahashi Korekiyo, introduced policies similar to those that Keynes had recommended in Britain. The Japanese currency was allowed to fall in value, helping Japanese companies, initially at least, to sell more abroad. Public spending was increased, which put money in people's pockets, allowing Japanese companies to sell more at home. The economy began to strengthen.

Unfortunately, the damage done to the countryside in 1929–31 had already had political consequences. The worst-hit areas were some of the army's main recruiting areas, and many of the men were outraged by the government's inability to improve matters. The armed forces were responsible to the emperor, not the government, allowing them to have their own policies. Their answer to the Depression, in the summer of 1931, was to complete the invasion of China's Manchuria and turn it into a virtual Japanese colony. With a single stroke, or so the army leaders claimed, they had created a new market for Japanese industry and extra room for the rapidly-growing Japanese population.

These two policies, the army's invasion of Manchuria, and the government's promotion of exports, helped to sour Japan's relations with other wealthy countries. Condemned for the invasion of Manchuria, Japan left the **League of Nations.** Other nations raised **tariffs** higher and higher in an attempt to keep out Japan's **exports.** By the mid-1930s, Japan's only friends were Germany and Italy.

> ## Method in his madness
>
> *There can be no flourishing economic life which has not before it and behind it a flourishing, powerful State as its protection . . . There can be no economic life unless behind this economic life there stands the determined political will of the nation absolutely ready to strike, and to strike hard . . .*
>
> Adolf Hitler, January 1932

A Japanese army column marches through a Manchurian town during the invasion of 1931.

Race and Gender

The Great Depression had an undeniable impact on how particular groups saw themselves and each other.

Racism in Europe

When times are hard, minorities often suffer the most. This was certainly true in many areas during the Depression. Hitler claimed that Jews were largely responsible for Germany's economic problems, and in 1935, his Nuremberg Laws stripped all German Jews of their citizenship and prohibited marriages between Jews and non-Jews. This persecution would intensify as the years passed and end in the the **Holocaust.**

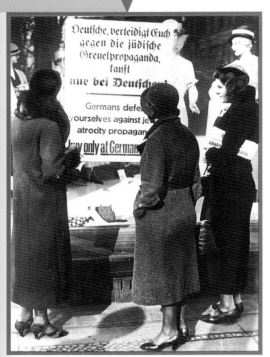

*Racist signs in the window of a Berlin store during a **boycott** of Jewish goods in **Nazi** Germany, 1933 were an omen of worse things to come.*

The Germans were the most violent culprits, but far from the only ones. Jews became convenient **scapegoats** throughout central and eastern Europe. In western countries like France, workers from eastern and southern Europe were much more likely to lose their jobs than those born in the area. The seriousness of such discrimination varied enormously from place to place. The British Union of **Fascists** tried hard to stir up racial hatred against the Jews in England, but with little success.

African Americans

The 1930s offered a mixed message to African Americans. As a whole, they suffered badly from the Depression. When companies cut jobs, African Americans were often the first to be fired, and the white-run unions frequently ignored them. As **tenant farmers** or domestic workers they didn't qualify for farm **subsidies** or unemployment **benefits.** There was no new anti-**lynching** law, and many states still had laws discriminating against them.

Aspects of U.S. life, like sports and the armed services, were still **segregated.** African-American neighborhoods in big cities were very poor and overcrowded. In March 1935, rioters in Harlem, an area in New York City, set out to destroy the local white-owned businesses.

There was some good news. President Roosevelt was reluctant to risk upsetting white voters by supporting African-American causes, but he did argue in favor of an anti-lynching bill. His wife Eleanor frequently

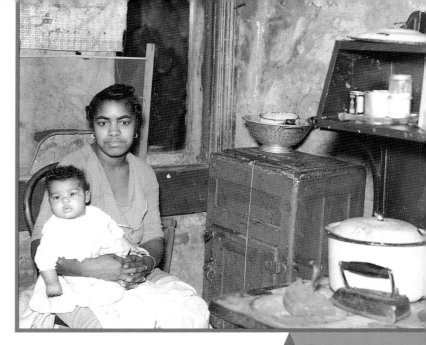

spoke out against the evils of racial discrimination. More significantly, it was written into New Deal programs that they had to be applied in a **nondiscriminatory** manner. Some historians have considered this an early step along the road to **civil rights.**

Times were difficult for women in the 1930s.

Women

On the whole, most women's lives barely changed from the 1920s to the 1930s. They looked after the children and home, and in many poorer countries they did most of the work in the fields as well.

In wealthier countries, the 1920s had seen a change in many women's expectations. This was reflected in many different ways, from voting rights to smoking in public. In the United States and western Europe, women were starting to claim equal rights in many areas. Partly in reaction to this, partly in reaction to the new circumstances of the Great Depression, the 1930s were a period of marking time where women's rights were concerned. Many women lost their jobs and their financial independence. Those who worked often had to suffer the mocking accusations of those who said they were taking away a man's job.

There was a shift back toward the belief that a woman's place was in the home, particularly in Germany. This trend was reinforced by another peculiarity of the 1930s—the new emphasis on home life for all the family, which accompanied the heyday of radio and the introduction of so many new household appliances, such as refrigerators and vacuum cleaners. Women who could afford such labor-saving devices certainly found housework easier than their mothers had, but in the world beyond their front door, there was little to cheer. Equality of pay, work, and opportunity often looked farther away in the 1930s than it had during the giddy optimism of the 1920s.

Arts and Entertainment

The Great Depression influenced the development of mass entertainment and the arts in many, often contradictory, ways. Entertainment that allowed people to "escape" their problems for a while became popular, while the more adventurous arts were often held back by a lack of money. Telling the stories of those caught up in the real-life Depression inspired some powerful music, novels, and films.

In the United States, one New Deal agency, the WPA, gave money to a variety of artists as part of its job creation program. Thousands of actors and musicians traveled across the country putting on plays and concerts; often for people who had rarely seen either before. Writers were paid to write plays for theater groups and practical books like tourist guides to U.S. cities and states. Painters decorated public buildings with murals and held exhibitions in schools. Photographers were employed to keep a record of life during the Depression. The historian Howard Zinn called this "an exciting flowering of arts for the people," and though the **subsidies** were withdrawn in 1939, many lives had been enriched.

Henry Fonda (center) starred as Tom Joad in John Ford's film The Grapes of Wrath, *based on Steinbeck's novel.*

From the 1920s to the 1930s

The 1930s weren't easy for innovators. The 1920s in the United States had produced a golden era of jazz, several ground-breaking novelists, and the **Harlem Renaissance** of African-American writers and musicians. Legendary artists like F. Scott Fitzgerald, William Faulkner, Langston Hughes, Bessie Smith, George Gershwin, Duke Ellington, Louis Armstrong ,and Hoagy Carmichael had all come to prominence. But in the 1930s improvisational jazz did not advance, there were few great new novelists, and the Harlem Renaissance faded.

The new golden era was Hollywood's. Through the years of the Great Depression, U.S. film stars became household names throughout the world. Other countries had film industries, but none could compete with Hollywood for volume and popularity. In theaters everywhere, people sat entranced by films that offered a picture of the way life should be, rather than the way it was in the grim depths of the Depression.

Mass spectator sports shared this boom in "escapist" entertainment, but this industry grew mostly within national boundaries. Few Europeans had heard of baseball's Babe Ruth, and even fewer Americans would have recognized the name of cricket's Don Bradman, though both could claim to be the finest in their game's history.

Singer and songwriter Woodie Guthrie's "dust- bowl ballads" portrayed the life of the poor.

Telling it like it was

Many writers did try to come to terms with the Great Depression, and their works offer a vivid picture of ordinary life in this period. Britain's George Orwell chronicled the era in two novels: *Down and Out in Paris and London* and *The Road to Wigan Pier*. The French author Louis-Ferdinand Céline covered much the same ground in his *Journey to the End of the Night*. John Steinbeck's novel *The Grapes of Wrath*, which was also filmed by director John Ford, is a harrowing account of one family's journey across the United States, from their dust-destroyed farm on the Great Plains to an equally difficult life as migrant fruit pickers in California. Woody Guthrie, the other U.S. artist most associated with the Depression, put the stories of such families into a series of songs, which became known as "the dust-bowl ballads." Steinbeck and Guthrie were both angry and accusing, but they also offered a portrait of how rich and wonderful life could be, even for those who seemed to have so little.

*Now as through the world I ramble,
I see lots of funny men,
Some will rob you with a six-gun,
and some with a fountain pen.*

*But as through this life you travel,
And as through your life you roam,
You won't never see an outlaw
Drive a family from their home.*
from Woody Guthrie's song *Pretty Boy Floyd*

You discover what it is like to be hungry. With bread and margarine in your belly you go out and look into the shop windows. Everywhere there is food insulting you in huge wasteful piles . . .
George Orwell in his 1930s reminiscences *Down and Out in Paris and London*

Economics and Politics

Keynesianism

One man who came out of the Great Depression with his reputation enhanced was the English economist John Maynard Keynes. He had been right in 1919 when he said that war **reparations** would do more harm than good. He was right again in 1931 when he said that traditional, budget-balancing policies would make the situation worse. Those countries that accidentally or by design followed the economic policies he recommended were the first to emerge from the Depression.

Keynes outlined his theories in a series of books: *The Economic Consequences of the Peace* (1919), *A Treatise on Money* (1930), and, most important of all, *The General Theory of Employment, Interest and Money* (1936). His central idea was that in the modern age, economies were not self-regulating. Governments needed to intervene to manage them, to learn how to use the controls at their disposal, and to keep them functioning at the best possible level. In times of depression they could start **public works** or have lower taxes, either of which would pump more **demand** into the economy—people would want to buy and spend—and so get it moving again. And, if the economy was overheating and **inflation** accelerating, they could slow it down by cutting back demand, taking the money out of people's pockets with higher taxes or higher **interest rates.**

Both Roosevelt's New Deal and Hitler's recovery plan for Germany involved the injection of public money to stimulate the economy, but such measures were seen as an emergency response to the Depression, not as a normal economic way of life. It was not until 1944 that Keynes's ideas would become the official policy of his own country. Most other countries would also adopt them in the postwar era.

This is the English economist John Maynard Keynes, who consistently argued for government intervention in the economy.

How economies work

*If the Treasury were to fill old bottles with banknotes, bury them at suitable depths in disused coal mines which are then filled up to the surface with town rubbish, and leave it to **private enterprise** [businesses not under state control] on well-tried principles of **laissez-faire** to dig the notes up again . . . there need be no more unemployment and, with the help of the repercussions, the real income of the community . . . would probably become a good deal larger than it actually is.*

J. M. Keynes, demonstrating that almost any government expenditure will create jobs and generate wealth, in his *General Theory of Employment, Book III*

Soviet planning

The levels of government intervention recommended by Keynes were considered "socialistic" by many, and with good reason. **Socialists** of all kinds had long argued for this, although they were usually more interested in promoting greater equality than the overall health of the economy. The Union of Soviet Socialist Republics, or Soviet Union, had taken this intervention to its logical extreme. Its political leaders and economic planners had assumed direct control of almost all economic activity, allowing very little free play for **market forces.**

When it became clear that interventionist policies were succeeding in fighting the Great Depression, many people in Europe and the United States looked to the experience of the Soviet Union with more interest. That country was affected by the collapse of world raw material prices that characterized the Depression, but its economy seemed to carry on growing regardless. There was no unemployment, no spread of **shanty towns,** no apparent despair.

The Soviet Union protected its economy by implementing Five-Year Plans.

How had the Soviet Union made itself immune to this economic virus that had incapacitated everyone else? Many began to wonder if the Soviet Union's Five-Year Plans were the answer. They seemed to make more sense than just leaving things to take care of themselves.

This was an understandable view. Security of employment, in particular, looked wonderful to those millions in the West who had been thrown out of work through no fault of their own. But it was also a very limited view. It would be years before most people outside the Soviet Union realized this. The truth was that such levels of government intervention always seemed to go hand in hand with both growing economic inefficiency and a gross neglect of other human rights.

Short-Term Effects: the Drift to War

The Great Depression did not inevitably lead to World War II, but its consequences certainly made conflict more likely. The period of intense economic hardship gave birth to nationalistic and militaristic governments in Germany, Japan, and most of the countries of eastern Europe. These governments created an atmosphere of confrontation both inside and outside their own countries, and deliberately brought to a head those national grievances that had been left simmering since the Versailles settlement of 1919. This was particularly true of Germany, where both the **Nazis** and the military were determined to rewrite the settlement in their own favor.

With the military playing such a prominent role in these regimes, **rearmament** was a popular policy. It not only helped their economies out of depression and made the new regimes more popular, but also made them more confident about getting their own way, particularly against weaker neighbors. When they succeeded in bullying one neighbor into submission, they were encouraged to try with another. This worried the other great powers who began rearming themselves. Sooner or later someone was bound to make a stand and then there would be war.

Adolf Hitler crossed into the Sudetenland region of Czechoslovakia, which had just been awarded to Germany at the Munich Conference.

Five economic blocs

The weakening of the world economy made each nation anxious to protect and, if possible, to expand existing markets for their own industries. Protecting markets involved building ever-higher **tariff** barriers to other nations' goods. By about 1935, the world economy had become roughly divided into five economic blocs. These were the sterling area, which included the British empire, Scandinavia, and parts of South America; the dollar area, or North and Central America and parts of South America; the yen area, with Japan and parts of China; the gold bloc, with the French and Italian empires; and the Deutschmark area, with Germany, central, and eastern Europe.

The high tariff walls surrounding these blocs made it hard for any country to sell outside its own bloc. Most countries found this difficult to accept, but Germany and Japan found it particularly annoying. They pointed out that the western powers already had their empires, so their need for new markets was not so desperate. They insisted that they too should be allowed to expand.

The Krupps factory at Essen, Germany prepares for war.

The Japanese expanded on the Asian mainland. They occupied Manchuria in 1931 and set out to conquer the rest of China in 1937. The Germans looked to eastern Europe, making a series of claims against Czechoslovakia and then Poland. Hitler's long-term aim was to find *lebensraum,* or "living space," further east, in what was then the Soviet Union.

All of the following developments were either caused by or quickened by the Great Depression: the rise of **fascism,** the spread of rearmament, the creation of tariff blocs, and the thrust to expand markets. They all encouraged the spread of aggressive nationalism. The Depression even blunted the **League of Nations'** one weapon against aggressive behavior. With everyone so desperate to sell, **economic sanctions** were impossible to enforce.

After World War II

The western powers came to understand that the political and economic policies they had pursued in the 1920s and 1930s had been partly to blame for the conditions that led to the outbreak of World War II. After defeating Germany and Japan, they tried to avoid repeating their past mistakes.

Dark times

What times are these when a conversation
About trees is almost a crime.
Because it includes a silence about so
many misdeeds!
from German playwright Bertolt Brecht's poem *To Posterity*

There were no **reparations** to hinder the postwar world economy, and the United States, rather than standing aloof as it had in 1918–19, took a leading role in the United Nations. Even more crucially, this time the Americans made sure that everyone would recover economically from the war and that no lasting grudges would be left to fester. Enormous amounts of money were poured into Europe and Japan, and the former enemies were soon readmitted to the prosperous family of nations.

Legacies of the Great Depression

The years of the Great Depression witnessed the greatest threat ever to the free enterprise, or **capitalist,** system. There were real fears of total collapse and revolution in the world's wealthiest countries. World War II brought an end to the Depression, but its effects are still being felt today. The changes it forced on governments did not vanish automatically when times improved, and the bitter memories of those who endured the greatest hardships were not wiped away by the steady growth of the postwar world. The legacy differed from continent to continent, but all were affected in some way.

One long-term consequence for the United States was the creation of the so-called "Imperial Presidency." In order to push through his economic and social policies, Roosevelt had stretched the power of the presidency and the **federal** government beyond previously accepted limits, and this trend continued during the war. In the second half of the century, many Americans believed that their country had a president with too much power, and "too much government" in general.

In August 1947, India celebrated its independence from Britain.

In western Europe, the most obvious reaction to the economic competition of the 1930s, and the military war which followed, was a steady growth of cooperation in the economic and political arenas. The European Economic Community demolished the **tariff** walls between national states and ushered in a new era of relative harmony.

In Asia, Africa, and Latin America the Depression had sown the seeds of discontent throughout Europe's overseas possessions, and the postwar world reaped the harvest. India and Indonesia became independent as early as the late 1940s, and by the end of the century, only a few isolated outposts of the **colonial** empires remained.

The Soviet Union, which had seemed immune to the effects of the Depression, probably benefited from it. For many people it looked as if the Soviets had succeeded where **capitalism** had failed. The propaganda boost lasted for years. If the Great

Depression had not occurred it would have been harder to take Soviet **communism** seriously as a method of running an economy.

Some consequences of the Depression affected everyone in the non-Soviet world. After the war, it was generally believed that tariff walls between national states were bad for business and political harmony. The western powers set up GATT—the General Agreement on Tariffs and Trade—to promote **free trade.** There were problems with this. The wealthier countries insisted on protecting some industries against outside competition. The poorer countries were rightly worried about their chances of survival in a trading "free-for-all." Such issues continue to generate disputes to this day.

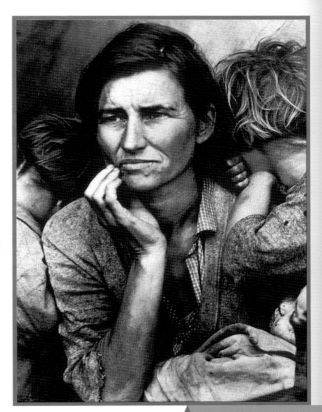

Dorothea Lange's famous photographs of migrant workers in California during the 1930s provide a moving pictorial record of the Great Depression.

The discrediting of laissez-faire

Inside the governments of many countries, the main legacy of the Depression was a distrust of do-nothing **laissez-faire** policies. For one thing, they didn't work. For another, they resulted in absurdities like the destruction of unsaleable food while people went hungry and the closure of factories that made goods people wanted. Such things seemed more than absurd, they seemed fundamentally wrong. By the end of the 1930s, the idea that economies ran themselves for the benefit of everyone had been almost completely discredited, and after World War II, governments were expected to intervene across the whole range of economic activities.

Governments took charge of economic forces, like taxes and **interest rates,** money supplies, and government borrowing levels—and used them to shift economic activity in whatever direction seemed necessary. The job of governments was to make sure that the economy was working in everyone's interests, and to provide a whole range of social **benefit** payments for people such as the elderly, the disabled, and the unemployed, who through no fault of their own were prevented from playing a full part in the economic process.

Making the connection

We have always known that heedless self-interest was bad morals. We now know that it is bad economics.

President Roosevelt, Second Inaugural Address, January 1937

Great Depression Time Line

1914 Beginning of World War I

1917 Russian Revolution

The United States enters the war

1918 End of World War I

1919 **Treaty of Versailles**

Founding of the **League of Nations**

1921 Warren Harding becomes U.S. president

German **reparations** bill decided

1923 French occupation of the Ruhr, Germany

The Great **Inflation** in Germany

Warren Harding dies in office, succeeded by Calvin Coolidge

1924 The Dawes Plan

1926 General Strike in Britain

1928 Share prices soar on **Wall Street,** in New York

1929 Herbert Hoover becomes U.S. president.

The Great Crash on Wall Street

1930 Worldwide rise of unemployment—prices, trade, and production fall

1931 Japanese invasion of Manchuria

National government formed in Britain

1932 British Empire conference in Ottawa, Canada

1933 Hitler comes to power in Germany

Roosevelt becomes president

First New Deal measures inacted

1934 Dust bowl conditions on the U.S. Great Plains

1935 Social Security Act in the United States

1937 Roosevelt's second inauguration

New **recession** in the United States

Japanese invasion of China

1938 Takeover of Austria and part of Czechoslovakia by Germany

1939 Outbreak of World War II

1945 End of World War II

Founding of the United Nations

1948 GATT formed

1957 European Economic Community set up by Treaty of Rome

Highs and Lows–Graphs

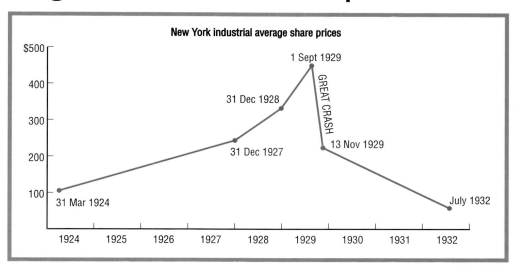

New York industrial average share prices

1 Sept 1929

GREAT CRASH

31 Dec 1928

31 Dec 1927

13 Nov 1929

31 Mar 1924

July 1932

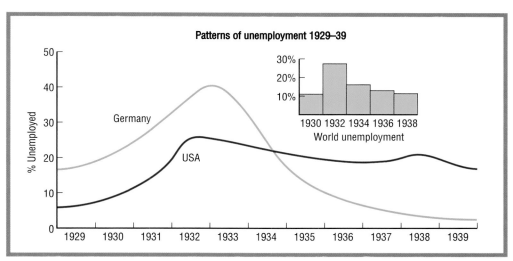

Patterns of unemployment 1929–39

% Unemployed

Germany

USA

World unemployment

More Books to Read

Nonfiction

Burg, David F. *The Great Depression.* New York: Facts on File, 1996.

Isaacs, Sally Senzell. *America in the Time of Franklin Delano Roosevelt.* Chicago: Heinemann Library, 1999.

Meltzer, Milton. *Brother, Can You Spare a Dime: The Great Depression of 1929–1933.* New York: Facts on File, 1990.

Fiction

Grote, JoAnn. *Black Tuesday.* Uhrichsville, OH: Barbour Publishing, Inc., 1999.

Johnson, Hilda S. *A Child's Diary—the 1930s.* Studley, Va.: The Wishing Room, 1988.

Steinbeck, John. *The Grapes of Wrath.* New York: Penguin, 1999.

Glossary

balanced budget situation when government spending does not exceed government income

bankrupt unable to pay debts

benefit payment made by a government to those who, for various reasons, are unable to work

boom period of sharp economic growth

boycott refusal to have any dealings with a business firm or other institution

broker professional buyer and seller of shares

capitalism free enterprise economic system, in which most business is privately owned and run

cash-crop crop grown for sale rather than consumption, often for export

civil rights rights of all people to equal treatment and economic opportunities

colony territory ruled by another, usually faraway, country

communism political system in which the state owns and controls the means of production

Congress lawmaking body of the United States made up of the Senate and the House of Representatives

credit money available for borrowing

demand in economics, what is both wanted by people and affordable

democracy government by the people or their elected representatives

Democratic Party in the United States, one of the two major political parties, usually more in favor of government intervention in the economy than the Republicans

dictatorship government controlled by an individual or a small group in which most people have no say

direct tax tax like income tax which takes more from wealthy individuals than poor

economic sanctions refusal to trade with another nation, either in one particular product or in all

export good or service sold to other countries

fascism dictatorial system of government that places the nation before the individual and uses violent means to put down any opposition

federal central government in the United States, based in Washington, D.C.

free market market unregulated or little regulated by government

free trade trade without charges for bringing goods across international borders

Harlem Renaissance literary and artistic movement in the early twentieth century named after an African-American neighborhood in New York

Holocaust murder of millions of people by Nazi Germany in 1942–45

Hundred Days special session of Congress early in Franklin Roosevelt's presidency when new legislation was quickly passed

hydroelectric power electricity generated by flowing water

imports goods or services bought from foreign countries

indirect tax tax that tends to penalize rich and poor by the same amount, most often hurting poorer individuals more

inflation increase in prices or increase in the supply of money, which leads to an increase in prices

interest rates levels at which borrowed money must be repaid

invest to put money into economic projects in the hope of making a profit

laissez-faire philosophy that opposes governments getting involved in their economies

League of Nations international organization set up after World War I to help settle disputes between nations

lynching execution without legal trial

malnutrition condition caused by a lack of enough healthy food

migrant someone with no home who moves from place to place in search of work

market forces workings of supply, or what is or is not available, and demand, or what is or is not wanted

mortgage loan taken out to buy a home, property, or business

Nazis German National Socialist Party, led by Adolf Hitler from 1921–1945

New York Stock Exchange New York marketplace where professionals sell percentages of businesses to individuals

nondiscriminatory applied in the same way to everyone

preferential access provision of lower charges for one nation's exports than another's

primary products raw materials like crops and minerals

private enterprise business not owned or controlled by government

propaganda promotion of ideas, often involving a selective version of the truth

proportional representation system of voting in which each party is represented in proportion to the votes it receives

protectionism use of tariffs to protect industry and agriculture from foreign competition

public work building operation organized and financed by the government

racism hatred of other races

rearmament increase in the production of weapons

recession economic downturn

reforestation replanting with trees

reparations payments to make amends for war damage

Republican Party in the United States, one of the two major political parties, usually less in favor of government intervention in the economy than the Democrats

scapegoat person blamed for other people's problems

segregated kept apart, usually applied to ethnic groups, such as African American and white communities in the United States

shanty town group of makeshift homes where living conditions are severely poor and unsanitary

share certificate that represents pieces of a business and that entitles the holders to a portion of any money the business makes after all the costs of running the business have been paid

socialism political system in which the production and distribution of goods are controlled by the state

speculator person who makes money by gambling on changes in the price of stocks and shares

stock money loaned to a company or government in return for a share in the profits

stock market place where stocks and shares are bought and sold

subsidy extra money given, usually by government, to help individuals or businesses

subsistence farmer farmer who grows food just for his or her own family's survival

tariff charge for bringing goods across international borders

tenant farmer farmer who does not own the land but pays a portion of crops he or she grows to the landowner

topsoil fertile top layer of soil

Treaty of Versailles document that officially ended World War I and that included very harsh terms for Germany

trust company that buys and sells shares for other individuals

unemployment insurance money paid by government to the unemployed on a regular basis

Wall Street center of New York's business district and site of its Stock Exchange.

Index